December 1, 1955

Rosa Parks
and Her Protest for
Civil Rights

Phillip Steele

A⁺

Smart Apple Media

First published by Cherrytree Press
(a member of the Evans Publishing Group)
327 High Street, Slough
Berkshire SL1 1TX, United Kingdom
Copyright © 2002 Evans Brothers Limited
This edition published under license from
Evans Brothers Limited. All rights reserved.

Designed by Neil Sayer, Edited by Louise John

Published in the United States by
Smart Apple Media
1980 Lookout Drive
North Mankato, MN 56003

U.S. publication copyright © 2003 Smart Apple Media
International copyright reserved in all countries. No part of this book may be
reproduced in any form without written permission from the publisher.
Printed in Hong Kong

Library of Congress Cataloging-in-Publication Data

Steele, Philip. Rosa Parks and her protest for civil rights / by Philip Steele.
p. cm. — (Dates with history) Summary: A simple introduction to the life of Rosa Parks and
her role in the efforts to gain equal rights for African Americans.
ISBN 1-58340-215-2
1. Parks, Rosa, 1913- —Juvenile literature. 2. African American women—Alabama—
Montgomery—Biography—Juvenile literature. 3. African Americans—Alabama—
Montgomery—Biography—Juvenile literature. 4. Civil rights workers—Alabama—
Montgomery—Biography—Juvenile literature. 5. Montgomery (Ala.)—Biography—Juvenile
literature. 6. African Americans—Civil rights—Alabama—Montgomery—History—20th
century—Juvenile literature. 7. Segregation in transportation—Alabama—Montgomery—
Juvenile literature. 8. Montgomery (Ala.)—Race relations—Juvenile literature. [1. Parks, Rosa,
1913- 2. Civil rights workers. 3. African Americans—Biography. 4. Women—Biography.] I.
Title. II. Series.

F334.M753 P3877 2002   323'.092—dc21   [B]   2002021025

9 8 7 6 5 4 3 2 1

Picture credits:
AFP: 26
Corbis: Front cover, 6, 9, 11, 16, 17, 20, 21, 24, 25, 27
Hulton Getty: 8, 10, 13, 14, 15, 22, 23
Topham Picturepoint: 12, 18, 19

Contents

Dreaming of a Fairer World

December 1955: Christmas is coming, the season of goodwill. Stores are beginning to put up colored lights and sparkling trees. This is Montgomery, state capital of Alabama, in the heart of the American South. The city made its name as a market for cotton, timber, and cattle, but it has grown in recent years.

Montgomery's sidewalks are busy this evening with workers returning home. Many of them are **African Americans**. Although they make up over a third of the city's population of 130,000, they are treated as second-class citizens by most of the whites who live there. Among the blacks is Rosa Parks, tired after a hard day's work at her sewing machine. She is a quiet, middle-aged woman, who until now hasn't stood out in the crowd.

Rosa Parks in the 1950s.

Rosa was born Rosa Louise McCauley in Tuskegee, Alabama, on February 4, 1913. She knew poverty and hard times at an early age. Her father was James McCauley, a carpenter and stonemason. Her mother was a teacher called Leona Edwards. Both were African Americans. Rosa was given a strict Christian upbringing in the African Methodist Episcopal Church.

At the Montgomery Industrial School for Girls, the 11-year-old Rosa was no rebel. She was serious, soft-spoken, and did as she was told. However, her parents did tell her about African-American history, and of their dreams for a fairer world.

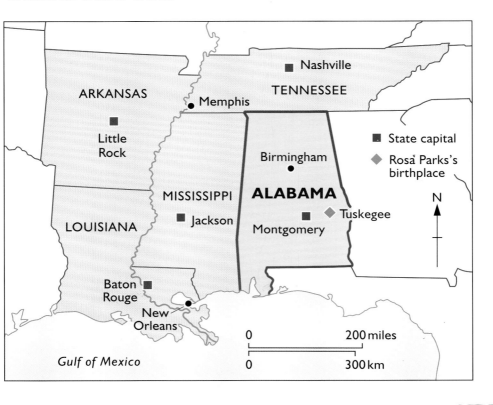

A map showing Alabama and neighboring southern states.

Rosa's Refusal

In 1932, Rosa married a barber called Raymond Parks. Raymond and Rosa shared a passion for social justice, and during this time both campaigned for the National Association for the Advancement of Colored People (NAACP). Through this organization, Rosa met both blacks and whites who were determined to bring about a fairer society.

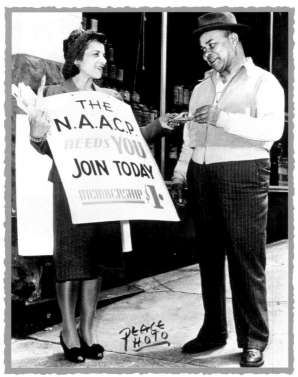

A woman recruits new members for the NAACP in the 1950s.

After work on December 1, 1955, Rosa boards the bus and buys a ticket. The front of the bus is reserved for whites. Blacks must sit at the back. Blacks are allowed to sit in the middle, but only if no whites are left standing. Rosa sits in the middle.

Rosa hates this **discrimination** against her people. Back in 1943 she had an argument with a **racist** bus driver over this. She now realizes that this same man, James F. Blake, is driving the bus this evening. At the third stop, a white man climbs aboard and demands a seat in the middle section. Driver Blake orders all the blacks in Rosa's row to stand. The others begin to obey—but Rosa refuses to move. Blake calls the police. When they arrive, they arrest Rosa. The prisoner goes peacefully, and is taken to the police station and fingerprinted. Some days later, she is fined $10.

The NAACP is angry that Rosa has been humiliated in this way and decides to **boycott** the public transportation system. Seventy-five percent of the city's bus passengers are black. Let the bus company see how they survive without these fares. The word spreads like wildfire among African Americans. Walk, arrange lifts, ride bicycles—but don't travel by bus!

Rosa Parks photographed sitting at the front of a bus after her protest in 1955.

A Change in the Law

Activists set up the Montgomery Improvement Association (MIA) to organize the protest. Its elected leader is the **pastor** of the Baptist church on Dexter Avenue, Dr. Martin Luther King, Jr. He is a captivating speaker, whom Rosa has already met. The MIA's demands are modest: that courtesy is shown to black passengers, that blacks no longer have to give up their seats, that the bus company hires black drivers.

Martin Luther King standing outside his church when he was pastor.

Martin Luther King and Glenn Smiley sit next to each other on a bus in 1956.

Rosa campaigns tirelessly and loses her job because of her efforts. Many African Americans are beaten up and arrested. King's home is bombed. But the boycott holds out until November 13, 1956, when the U.S. Supreme Court finally rules that Alabama's transportation laws are illegal. On December 21, 1956, Martin Luther King and a white minister named Glenn Smiley sit side by side on a bus. Rosa has won her battle.

Rosa Parks had started a new chapter in the story of African Americans and their campaign for civil rights. What lay behind her brave protest? What was the history of African Americans, and why were they treated so unfairly?

Out of Slavery

Slavery has been common throughout history. Slaves are people who are bought and sold like property and forced to work for no wages. Europeans took part in the West African slave trade from the 1500s, shipping slaves to the new lands of the Americas. The slaves were kept in chains, and thrown overboard if they became sick.

A rich landowner buying black slaves.

The slaves who survived the Atlantic crossing were landed on the Caribbean islands or on the North American mainland. Individuals were sold and branded like cattle and forced to work on large farming estates, called **plantations**. They toiled in the hot sun, hoeing or harvesting cotton.

Punishments were harsh, with slaves being whipped, hanged, and even burned alive. Most white people at that time believed that whites were superior to blacks. However, some whites did recognize that these beliefs were **immoral**. After the U.S. became independent from Britain (1775–83), the northern states abandoned the use of slave labor, but this did not happen in the South.

Black slaves picking cotton in the fields of Texas in 1800.

Britain halted the Atlantic slave trade in 1807 and abolished slavery throughout its huge empire, including the Caribbean region, in 1833. In the same year, the American Anti-Slavery Society called for the **abolition** of slavery throughout the United States.

In 1861, the northern and southern states engaged in a terrible **civil war**. The Union (northern) side supported the end of slavery. The southern Confederacy—first set up in Montgomery, Alabama—supported slavery. About 179,000 African-American troops fought for the Union. In 1865, the Union finally won, and slavery was abolished.

Segregation and Terror

After the Civil War, freed slaves looked forward to a bright future, but once the northern troops had withdrawn from the South, old injustices were re-created.

In 1888, the first segregation laws were passed in Mississippi, and blacks were no longer able to mix with whites. Other laws made it impossible for most blacks to qualify to vote in elections. These became known as "Jim Crow" laws, after a mocking dance called "Jump, Jim Crow," performed by "blacked-up" white entertainers.

The Rex Theatre in Mississippi, which was segregated under the "Jim Crow" laws.

In 1866, a white racist terror group was founded, called the Ku Klux Klan. Its members murdered and tortured thousands of blacks. In 1915, the Klan was revived, attracting new members across the U.S. Rosa Parks's childhood was haunted by terrifying "Klansmen" marching up and down her street, threatening black families.

Blacks in the South were little better off than in the days of slavery. Many lived in poor country shacks with few possessions. The cotton fields offered tough, blistering, poorly paid work. Rosa picked cotton as a child, for 50 cents a day. Many poor whites were little better off than the blacks. During the 1930s, both peoples suffered greatly during a period of severe unemployment, known as the Great Depression.

Cloaked and hooded members of the Ku Klux Klan group standing in front of a fiery cross—one of their symbols.

This ended with the Second World War (1939–45). Although the war was being fought against German racists, black troops still suffered from discrimination in the U.S. armed forces.

The Struggle for Black Rights

African-American campaigns for civil rights had already been going on for 50 years or more when Rosa Parks made her protest in 1955. The NAACP had been founded as early as 1909. In 1934, an African-American Muslim called Elijah Muhammad had set up a black separatist movement known as the Nation of Islam.

Paul Robeson was a football star, a lawyer, a world-famous singer, an actor, and a movie star.

After the Second World War, black rights were championed by a remarkable African American called Paul Robeson. In the 1950s, Robeson lost work as the U.S. government accused him of being a **communist** troublemaker. The same accusation would soon be leveled against Rosa Parks during the bus boycott.

In August 1955, Rosa Parks was shocked and saddened by the murder of a black teenager called Emmett Till. Emmett had come down from Chicago to visit relatives in Money, Mississippi. He boasted to friends that he had dated a white girl back home. They dared him to talk to the white woman who ran the local store, Carolyn Bryant. When he called her "baby," she complained to her husband that Emmett had spoken without due respect.

Emmett was seized by Carolyn's husband and brother, tortured, shot, and thrown into the Tallahatchie River. When the case came to trial, the Ku Klux Klan set out to **intimidate** witnesses. An all-white **jury** found the murderers "not guilty."

Black teenager Emmett Till in 1955.

Death Threats and Protests

The civil rights movement was growing across the U.S., with the support of young blacks and whites. Blacks were encouraged to register to vote. A growing threat came from racist White Citizens' Councils. These were made up of "respectable" citizens, but they did everything they could to oppose justice for blacks. In 1957, Rosa Parks received one death threat too many. She and Raymond moved north to Detroit, Michigan.

Members of the sheriff's mounted posse patrol the front of the bus station in Montgomery, Alabama, following the arrival of a group of "Freedom Riders."

In 1960, black students in Nashville, Tennessee, sat down at a department-store lunch counter that was reserved for whites. They refused to move. This was just the first of many "sit-in" protests. In 1961, two buses of blacks and whites set out from Washington, D.C., for New Orleans. They wanted to challenge segregation on interstate buses. In Alabama these "Freedom Riders" were firebombed and beaten up. The state governor took no action. Eventually the U.S. attorney general, Robert Kennedy, stepped in to enforce interstate bus **integration**.

Another civil rights battlefield was education. Segregation in schools had been banned in 1954, but this law was ignored in the South.

A black student is protected by a U.S. marshal as she walks to college.

In 1957, black pupils admitted to the all-white high school in Little Rock, Arkansas, were met by an angry white mob and paratroopers had to be called in to protect them.

"I Have a Dream . . ."

The year 1963 saw the civil rights movement at its height, but it was a year of tragedy. On June 12, Medgar Evers, NAACP secretary in Mississippi, was gunned down in front of his home. He had campaigned for voter registration and for the boycott of whites-only stores. It was he who had helped organize witnesses in the Emmett Till murder trial.

During the 1963 Freedom March, King spoke about discrimination in both northern and southern states.

Evers's murder led to a meeting between civil rights workers and U.S. President John F. Kennedy, who now called for new laws. On November 22, "JFK," who was idolized by many progressive young Americans, was assassinated in Dallas, Texas. To this day, nobody is sure why.

On June 23, 1963, Rosa Parks, who by now was a very prominent figure among civil rights activists, and Martin Luther King led a Great March to Freedom through the streets of Detroit. Two months later, Rosa Parks joined the vast stream of people marching on Washington, D.C.

Some 300,000 people gathered at the center of the capital. Rosa was angry that no women were asked to address the crowd, but Martin Luther King made a very moving speech, which went down in history. He began with the words "*I have a dream . . .*"

In 1965, Rosa Parks gave up her sewing job and started to work for John Conyers, an African American who had been elected congressman.

In March of that year, another march started in Alabama, from Selma to Montgomery. The marchers were calling for black voting rights to be protected. But the peaceful marchers were brutally attacked by police and state troopers. Rosa was anguished. She flew to Montgomery, where, with Martin Luther King, she addressed 25,000 protestors.

In his famous "I have a dream" speech, Martin Luther King described his vision of an America free from racial injustice.

Black Power

Dr. Martin Luther King was by now known and respected around the world. In 1964, he was awarded the **Nobel Peace Prize**. Despite all the violence directed at him, King never returned the hatred, and campaigned using only nonviolent methods. On April 4, 1968, King was assassinated. He was killed by a white racist called James Earl Ray, in Tennessee.

On June 5, another assassination shocked the U.S. The victim was Robert Kennedy, brother of JFK and supporter of the civil rights campaign. Rosa Parks was shattered by the loss of two men whom she had so admired.

The National Guard patrols the streets after the Detroit riots in 1967 (see page 23).

However, the nonviolent methods preached by Martin Luther King had been successful. Major political reforms were brought in during the 1960s, but young blacks were growing restless. Political change had brought no **economic** benefits. Blacks still lived in poor housing. They still could not get decent jobs. They were expected to fight for their country in the Vietnam War, but at home they were still **harassed** by the police.

Between 1964 and 1967, there were riots in cities across the U.S. Many people died, hundreds were injured, thousands were left homeless. Rosa Parks sharply condemned the rioting, even if she understood its causes. However, many young blacks declared that violence had to be met with violence. Many called for revolution and **Black Power**. An armed revolutionary organization called the Black Panthers was founded, and there was even a Black Power protest at the 1968 Olympic Games in Mexico.

Malcolm X was murdered by former associates in 1965.

Rosa Parks, the gentle Christian activist, belonged to a different generation. But even she respected one of the new leaders, Malcolm X, when she met him. He founded a new Organization of Afro-American Unity, calling for peace.

Change for the Better . . . and Worse

Many of the older civil rights activists were bitterly disappointed by the violent mood of the late 1960s and '70s, but they understood how young African Americans felt angry and frustrated.

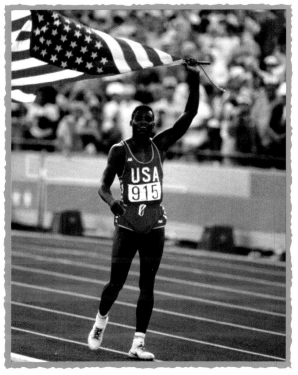

Black athlete Carl Lewis gained the respect of the nation when he won four gold medals in the 1984 Olympic Games.

The 1980s and '90s did see a great change in public attitudes in the U.S. Black stars were now seen in films and on television. Black musicians, athletes, poets, and writers were respected by both blacks and whites. African Americans entered politics and business. By 1989, there was even a black state governor in Mississippi. A national holiday in January was declared to honor Martin Luther King.

For all these gains, there were worrying signs that the goals of Rosa Parks and other civil rights campaigners had still not been met.

Police officer Powell (right) with his family during his trial for assaulting Rodney King.

In 1991, a video recording showed police officers kicking and beating up a black motorist, Rodney King, in Los Angeles. The policemen were acquitted, although a retrial found two of them guilty. In 1998, a disabled black man from the South, James Byrd, was chained to the back of a truck and dragged along the road until he died.

The Ku Klux Klan still existed, only its members now wore suits and ties, and talked politely to the television cameras, just like respectable politicians. Racists preached hatred over the Internet. Economic inequality still existed, too. In the U.S., a black American was twice as likely to be unemployed as a white.

Never Give Up

Rosa Parks may have been quiet and forgiving, but she was also tough and unswerving. She never gave up her ideals and still urged people onward toward a fairer society. In 1977, Raymond, her husband, died of cancer and from 1979 on, she had to care for her elderly mother.

The year 1987 saw the founding of the Parks Institute, which encouraged young people to discover self-respect and confidence. In 1994, Rosa was mugged in her home by a young black intruder, but she battled on. In 1996, she was awarded the Presidential Medal of Freedom.

During her later years, Rosa Parks was helped through difficult times by her friend and fellow activist, Elaine Steele (left).

By 1998, Rosa's health was becoming poor. However, she had a great tonic in 1999, when Nelson Mandela visited Detroit. Mandela was a black South African who had been jailed in 1964 for battling against injustice in his own country. Not released until 1990, he became South Africa's first black, democratically elected president.

In 2000, a museum was named after Rosa Parks, by the spot in Montgomery where she was arrested in 1955. However, Rosa's true memorial remains her message— never give up the struggle for freedom and justice.

Nelson Mandela embraces Rosa Parks as the two veteran campaigners meet in 1999.

Timeline

1500s Start of the transatlantic slave trade.

1807 Britain halts transatlantic slave trade.

1833 Britain ends slavery in its empire (including Canada and the Caribbean); American Anti-Slavery Society calls for abolition in the United States.

1861–65 Civil War, abolition of slavery.

1866 Founding of the Ku Klux Klan.

1884 Start of the "Jim Crow" laws.

1909 Founding of the National Association for the Advancement of Colored People (NAACP).

1913 *February 4:* Rosa Louise McCauley (Parks) is born.

1932 Rosa McCauley marries Raymond Parks.

1934 Founding of the Nation of Islam movement.

1941 United States enters the Second World War.

1955 *August 13:* Murder of Emmett Till.

1955 *December 1:* Rosa Parks is arrested for her bus protest.

1956 *November 13:* U.S. Supreme Court rules against bus segregation laws.

1956 *December 21:* Bus desegregation enforced in Montgomery, Alabama.

1957	*July:* Death threats force Rosa Parks to move to Detroit.
1957	*September:* Riots at Little Rock, Arkansas, as black pupils try to enter high school.
1960	Lunch-counter sit-ins, Nashville, Tennessee.
1961	The "Freedom Riders" challenge segregation.
1963	*June 12:* Murder of Medgar Evers.
1963	*June 23:* Great March to Freedom, Detroit.
1963	*August 28:* Martin Luther King addresses 300,000 in Washington, D.C.
1963	*November 22:* Assassination of President John F. Kennedy.
1965	*February 21:* Malcolm X is assassinated in Harlem, New York.
1965	*March 7:* Start of the Selma-to-Montgomery freedom march.
1965	*August:* Violent riots in Watts, Los Angeles.
1966	Rise of the Black Panthers and the Black Power movement.
1967	*July:* Violent riots in Detroit.
1968	*April 4:* Assassination of Martin Luther King.
1968	*June 5:* Assassination of Robert Kennedy.
1987	Founding of the Parks Institute.
1996	Rosa Parks is awarded the Presidential Medal of Freedom.
1999	Rosa Parks meets Nelson Mandela in Detroit.

Glossary

abolition Getting rid of a custom or law.

African Americans Americans whose ancestors came from Africa.

Black Power A movement calling for people of African descent to rise up and seize power for themselves.

boycott To make a protest by refusing to deal with someone or to use their services.

civil war A war between two armies within a single country, as happened with the U.S. 1861–65.

communist Believing that the working classes should seize power and take control of the economy and government.

discrimination Treating one group of people differently from another.

economic Having to do with the economy, the way in which money, employment, and trade are organized.

harassed Bothered or tormented without end.

immoral Going against ideas of what is right or just.

integration Making sure that all people are included in something —the opposite of segregation.

intimidate To scare people off from doing something, to terrorize them.

jury A group of people called in to decide guilt or innocence in a court case.

Nobel Peace Prize An international prize that is awarded to people who have helped make the world a more peaceful place.

pastor A clergyman, minister, or priest.

plantations Large farming estates that produce a crop such as cotton or sugar cane.

racist Someone who believes that one race is superior to another.

Index